What people are saying about

The Guided Life

This is a gem of a book. *The guided life* is central to the Quakers and to all of us who feel God gathering us in community. Mixing personal insights and examples from the Quaker tradition, this book offers a rich feast of spiritual insight.
Ben Pink Dandelion, Honorary Professor of Quaker Studies, University of Birmingham

This is surely one of the best descriptions of the Quaker way of life we have. It explains so clearly the human experience on which it is based, the practical exercises we can undertake to follow it, and the outcome of following it in a wholesome, joyful life that is shared with other people.
Rex Ambler, author of *The Quaker Way: A Rediscovery*

At a time when religion is often the source of considerable division, Craig Barnett has written a beautiful book which describes with undogmatic assurance the gentle power of the Quaker Way and the strength of the Inward Guide. Those familiar with Quakerism, and those desiring to know more, will learn how this Way of worship can strengthen, heal and nurture both the individual and community.
Gerald Hewitson, author of *Journey into Life: Inheriting the story of early Friends*

QUAKER QUICKS

The Guided Life

Finding purpose in troubled times

QUAKER QUICKS

The Guided Life

Finding purpose in troubled times

Craig Barnett

CHRISTIAN ALTERNATIVE
BOOKS

Winchester, UK
Washington, USA

JOHN HUNT PUBLISHING

First published by Christian Alternative Books, 2019
Christian Alternative Books is an imprint of John Hunt Publishing Ltd.,
No. 3 East St., Alresford, Hampshire SO24 9EE, UK
office@jhpbooks.com
www.johnhuntpublishing.com
www.christian-alternative.com

For distributor details and how to order please visit the 'Ordering' section on our website.

Text copyright: Craig Barnett 2018

ISBN: 978 1 78535 896 8
978 1 78535 897 5 (ebook)
Library of Congress Control Number: 2018955412

A CIP catalogue record for this book is available from the British Library.

Design: Stuart Davies

UK: Printed and bound by CPI Group (UK) Ltd, Croydon, CR0 4YY
US: Printed and bound by Thomson-Shore, 7300 West Joy Road, Dexter, MI 48130

We operate a distinctive and ethical publishing philosophy in all areas of our business, from our global network of authors to production and worldwide distribution.

Contents

Chapter 1

The Guided Life

The world needs guided men and women, not guided missiles.

When I read this message on a sign outside a Quaker Meeting House many years ago, I was intrigued by the idea of a guided life. What might it mean to be 'guided', by what or whom? It was only much later, when I began to discover some of the little-known depths of Quaker spiritual teaching, that I realised here was a religious tradition that had made the cultivation of the guided life the focus of its practice for over three centuries.

The Quaker way is not concerned with the question 'what should I believe?' which is usually of little practical significance. Instead, it is a response to the far more pressing and vital question, one that we are all forced to answer in some fashion – 'how shall I live?'

In the aftermath of the English Civil War, the first Quakers discovered a source of insight, power and guidance within themselves, which they called by various names, including 'the Inward Guide', 'the Light', 'the Seed', 'the Inward Teacher' and 'the Inward Christ'. Over centuries, the Religious Society of Friends has developed and refined a tradition of spiritual practice that can help to nurture a conscious connection to this source of inward guidance.

This Inward Teacher is present in all people, cultures and traditions. The Quaker way has developed within the wider Christian tradition, and draws on the imagery and language of the Bible, but it does not claim any exclusive or privileged status for Christianity over other spiritual traditions. The Inward Guide goes by many names and is understood in many ways, but it is equally available to everyone who is willing to listen and respond.

Throughout their history, Quakers have developed practices for 'discerning' the guidance of the Spirit of God in their personal and community lives. Spiritual discernment is experienced as a form of perception, by which we come to sense the action of the divine life within our own feelings, thoughts and experience. It requires us to become sensitive to 'the promptings of love and truth' within us, that through long experience have been recognised as signs of the activity of the Inward Guide. The heart of all Quaker practice is a simple attentiveness to the truth of our experience. This is what the Quaker writer Patricia Loring has described as a 'listening spirituality', explaining that:

> If we are listening for the will of God, it behooves us to listen with our hearts, the marrow of our bones and our whole skin, as well as with our ears.

It is not necessary to be a member of the Religious Society of Friends to make use of Quaker practices, although it is a great help to be part of a community that discerns together, that can test and support an individual's sense of being 'led' to action, and that works together to become more faithful to the guidance of the Spirit. The human capacity to distinguish between divine guidance and our own desires and obsessions is notoriously unreliable. People who are convinced of their own divine mission and God-given authority can commit terrifying actions. It is for just this reason that the Quaker tradition has developed communal practices for testing individual leadings, so that the collective experience and varied insights of the community becomes a resource for individual discernment and a safeguard against destructive enthusiasms. Even with the support of a community, this way of learning to trust in an inward source of guidance does not come with any guarantees. The Quaker tradition does not promise the illusory security of certainty, but

2

spiritual practices for working with and through the uncertainty that is a necessary part of being human.

The Quaker way is grounded in a conviction that we cannot surrender responsibility for our own lives by submission to authority or conformity to any group. Instead, we need to discover the source of our own inward authority, which, if we place our trust in it, may lead us in unexpected directions. It is this trust in the mysterious springs of life within that Quakers understand as 'faith'. Rather than a set of beliefs or principles, a lived faith in the Inward Guide is a willingness to loosen our grip on the course of our life, surrendering to an inner process of healing and transformation.

This experience of being inwardly guided serves the deepest needs of our nature, but it does not serve our comfort, self-image or security. It often challenges us deeply, pushing us to move beyond security and exposing our cherished illusions about ourselves. Ultimately, it is given for the healing of the world, through us. The Quaker way challenges us to accept that each of us is needed. This means taking our lives seriously enough to accept that the choices we make are not just arbitrary preferences. Each of us has something unique to offer the world. It may be simply the quality of our presence in our family or workplace, or our willingness to be alongside a vulnerable person, but there is something that only we can do in this particular time and place. The Quaker experience has been that when we give our consent to being led, we will be guided, invited and sustained to fulfil the unique purpose that has been given to us.

Quakers have a long reputation as reformers, campaigners and rebels against slavery, militarism, nuclear weapons and homophobia. Where these activities have been most faithful to the roots of Quaker spirituality, they have not been motivated by high-minded idealism or righteous fury. Instead, they have grown from the rich soil of Quaker worship and collective discernment, which gradually sensitises the heart, mind and will to the divine compassion for the world.

The Quaker way is not an earnest striving for ethical absolutes. It is guided by a subtle and sensitive perception of what is, rather than fixed convictions about what ought to be. Quaker discernment is not concerned with general moral principles, but with each person's particular calling at this specific point in their life. It is not up to us to impose our idea of the perfect society. Our responsibility is simply to be attentive to the guidance that is available specifically for us, in the depths of our experience, and to be ready to respond to it. This is the calling to 'return home to within' that is expressed in the richly poetic language of the seventeenth century by the early Quaker Francis Howgill:

> Return, return to Him that is the first Love, and the first-born of every creature, who is the Light of the world ... Return home to within, sweep your houses all, the groat is there, the little leaven is there, the grain of mustard-seed you will see, which the Kingdom of God is like; ... and here you will see your Teacher not removed into a corner, but present when you are upon your beds and about your labour, convincing, instructing, leading, correcting, judging and giving peace to all that love and follow Him.

Through the practice of attentive discernment, generations of Quakers have found themselves, to their own surprise, called to live among distant peoples, to welcome strangers into their homes, or to challenge unjust laws, as well as many much quieter activities in daily life. In modern societies that are often deadened by apathy and absence of purpose, these people have discovered a desire to nurture the seed of life they have encountered within, which has made even their struggles and hardships full of significance and sources of gratitude and joy.

Chapter 2

The Inward Guide

Therefore the main thing in religion is to keep the conscience pure to the Lord, to know the guide, to follow the guide, to receive from him the light whereby I am to walk; and not to take things for truths because others see them to be truths, but to wait till the spirit makes them manifest to me.
(Isaac Penington, 1660)

When our family moved house last summer, Kate and I worked out that it was our thirteenth move in the twenty years we have been together. This is probably rather extreme, but it is far from unusual for people to change house, city, job or profession several times during their lives.

In most developed countries, we now share a common culture of continuous and unpredictable change. We may need to repeatedly move long distances for study or work, and few of us can count on a life-long occupation, as entire industries are transformed during our working lives. Most large organisations in private and public sectors are subject to regular restructuring, job losses or changes of role, relocations or redundancies. Many occupations that formerly offered secure employment have been outsourced to contractors, and employees forced into contracts with irregular hours and little job security. Over recent years this radical uncertainty has come to affect even formerly secure areas such as public services, local government and higher education. Insecurity and unpredictability increasingly affect the lives of the majority, instead of being confined to the least privileged groups in society.

A friend is facing yet another reorganisation in his workplace, which will lead to further redundancies. Knowing that he will have to re-apply for his existing job, should he apply for voluntary redundancy? Should he look for a job in a related industry, or try retraining in something completely different? Rational calculation can only take us so far in situations like this, which quickly lead into fundamental questions of meaning, value and purpose. 'What kind of work do I want to do?' 'What is a worthwhile use of my time, effort and ability?' 'What should I do with my life?' These are not questions that can be answered by the application of any general principle, and yet they demand a practical, and sometimes an urgent response.

Experiences such as this point towards the need for reliable approaches that can help us to live through times of profound change, to cope with uncertainty, and to discover the sources of deep motivation in our own lives. The Quaker way has developed a tradition of spiritual practices for discovering an inward source of guidance. These are practices that have been tested by many generations, through more than three centuries of enormous social, political and cultural change, and are still relied on by Quakers throughout the world to navigate the challenges and complexities of modern societies.

Quaker Worship

In the social and cultural chaos of the immediate aftermath of a devastating civil war in England, the first Quakers developed a new spiritual practice for the worship of God, which they described as 'waiting in the light'.

> The first that enters into the place of your meeting ... turn in thy mind to the light, and wait upon God singly, as if none were present but the Lord; and here thou art strong. Then the next that comes in, let them in simplicity of heart sit down and turn in to the same light, and wait in the spirit; and so all the rest coming in, in the fear of the Lord, sit down in pure stillness and silence of all flesh, and wait

in the light ...
(Alexander Parker, 1660)

This form of worship does not involve following a prescribed ritual, or reciting a set form of words. It is the deliberate turning of our attention towards the 'Inward Light'; the quality of awareness that reveals to us our deepest insights and motivations.

One of the discoveries made by the first practitioners of Quaker worship was the experience of a state of consciousness that will show us the reality of our own life, if we allow it to. This inner capacity that reveals to us what is going on beneath our usual level of awareness is what Quakers call the 'Inward Light'. The Light is what enables us to see; it is a faculty of illumination and self-revelation that enables us to 'get a sight of ourselves', to recognise the truth of our own condition. Quakers have traditionally understood the Inward Light as a divine gift of spiritual perception, shining into our consciousness to reveal to us our true nature.

In this place of awareness, we 'stand still'. Instead of running away into distractions, we simply wait to see what is revealed to us in the depths of our own awareness. People who have practised the Quaker way throughout history have found that what the Inward Light reveals to us is rarely flattering. It is usually easy for us to find excuses for our own actions and reasons to blame others for conflicts or difficulties, but the Inward Light is not subject to our self-justifying strategies. Gradually, the process of simply sitting in attentive stillness tends to reveal the more hidden corners of ourselves, including the emotions and attitudes that we would prefer not to recognise, and the ways that we habitually act to undermine ourselves or others.

Experiences such as this are inevitably uncomfortable and often unwelcome. The fear of encountering our own darkness can deter us from spiritual practices that threaten to expose us to ourselves. But the promise of Quaker worship is that 'the same light that reveals your darkness will lead you out of it'. The same Inward Light or capacity for awareness that reveals our areas of shame, darkness and weakness, has the power to heal and transform them, and to lead us into new ways of feeling and acting. The Light 'shows us our darkness and leads us to new life'.

The practice of silent attention is not unique to Quakers – it has much in common with other traditions such as Buddhist and Hindu meditation and Christian contemplative prayer. The unusual insight of the Quaker way is that this practice is not limited to religious specialists. It can be employed by ordinary people, in the midst of daily life, without special training, sophisticated theory or a monastic lifestyle.

Quaker worship is a collective practice. Times of individual prayer or meditation are important spiritual disciplines for Quakers, but worship is practised as a community. Quakers early on discovered the extraordinary power of 'group mysticism' – the capacity of the gathered community to encounter a shared depth of stillness and an electric sense of divine presence. This quality of mutual kindling was described by the early Quaker Isaac Penington as 'like an heap of fresh and living coals, warming one another insomuch that a great strength, freshness and vigour of life flows into all'.

Perhaps because of this mutually reinforcing quality of collective worship, Quakers have usually dispensed with extensive training in meditative techniques. They have traditionally avoided prescribing detailed instructions for how to practise worship; trusting in the power of the gathered meeting to draw everyone into awareness of the Light. Over recent years, forms of guided meditation known as 'Experiment with Light' have also been developed, as a more structured process to help people to develop their experience of the Inward Light. (See the Appendix for a description of Experiment with Light.)

In Quaker worship it is expected that new insights may come

to anyone in the community, whatever their age or experience, and that they will be listened to as potential bearers of divine guidance. Anyone who takes part in a Quaker Meeting for Worship may be led by the Spirit to speak spontaneously to the meeting, to pass on whatever insights or guidance they have received. This reflects the Quaker emphasis on worship as a preparation for, and a source of guidance towards action. The aim of Quaker worship is not to find inner peace, comfort, absorption in God or freedom from an illusory ego. Its purpose is to encounter the source of inward transformation that may inspire and lead us to act; to speak in a Meeting for Worship, to make some change in our own lives, or to work for change in our community or society.

When I sit in worship, I begin with a process of becoming aware of my breathing and posture, and the presence of the others in the meeting room; letting go of thoughts and distractions to settle into a calm and receptive attitude. It soon becomes clear that distractions are not so easily let go of, as repetitive thoughts circle around to return again and again. Quite often a whole meeting can go by like this, without any apparent benefit. At other times, instead of random thoughts, an image or idea begins to take shape and gather significance. This might be prompted by what someone has said, or it may arise by itself, without any apparent connection to what I was thinking or feeling when I first sat down. Occasionally, I feel a growing impulse to speak, and words start to form themselves into a message for the meeting. This is often accompanied by a quickened heartbeat and a feeling of increased energy. Sometimes this feeling will fade away before I have become clear about how and when to speak. At other times, I find myself standing up, and try to communicate as best I can the message that has come to me in the silence.

In some meetings, as distractions fall away for a while, I meet with powerful emotions of sadness, grief, or shame that are usually buried beneath the surface. On a few, precious occasions, sinking down beneath the routine thoughts and anxieties, painful emotions and regrets, I have found myself held and surrounded by a healing Presence that seems to underlie all the suffering and confusion of the world, and to unite me with the rest of the meeting and with people everywhere. When this experience is shared by most or all of those present in a Meeting for Worship, there is a profound sense of being united in the Spirit that Quakers refer to as a 'gathered meeting':

> a meeting where the silence is as soft as velvet, as deep as a still pool; a silence where words emerge, only to deepen and enrich that rich silence, and where Presence is as palpable and soft as the skin of a peach; where the membrane separating this moment in time and eternity is filament-fine.
>
> (Gerald Hewitson, *Journey into Life*)

In the profound stillness of Quaker worship, we can experience something of the multifaceted, multiple aspects of God within. There is the peaceful, healing, sustaining presence of God that might envelope us unexpectedly, in a deep sense of connection with each other and the world around us. There is also the disturbing, challenging and energising face of God, as we become increasingly sensitised to the lives of others and the world around us. We have met this aspect of the Inward Guide when some person or situation seems to speak directly to us, to call our name and to require a response.

Leadings

Throughout their history, Quakers have found that through their encounter with the mysterious source of inward life, they have been moved into specific kinds of action. Quakers recognise these inward promptings to act as 'leadings of the Spirit', or expressions of divine purpose. It is through the leadings of the

Inward Guide that we discover possibilities for our lives that we might never have thought possible. A leading might be experienced as a subtle inward 'nudge', a sudden insight, or as a response of affirmation to outward circumstances that seem to fall into place to open a way forward.

In the early 1990s, I encountered the voice of the Inward Guide in response to the great numbers of homeless young people begging on the streets of Manchester. Where I had previously walked past homeless people relatively undisturbed, suddenly I was 'struck to the heart', in a way that demanded a response. I started volunteering and then working for the Big Issue magazine, as it was just getting started outside London. This was an experience with far-reaching implications for the course of my future life that I hadn't planned and could not have foreseen.

This kind of experience, which can result in very different kinds of action according to people's own circumstances, is a common outcome of Quaker worship. The regular practice of waiting in the Light gradually acts to dissolve our barriers of indifference, leaving us increasingly tender and sensitive to the reality of the world around us. People who persevere with this discipline of opening themselves to the Light find their inner resistances gradually worn away, able to see with fresh eyes the world and their place in it. They discover the inward presence of a Spirit of compassion that moves them into a passionate engagement with the world, whether in dramatic actions or the quieter, faithful commitments of daily life.

The Guide is described as 'inward' because it is experienced intimately in our inmost feelings, thoughts and perceptions, but it is not purely individual. We do not each have our own, unique guide or light, which is independent of everyone else's. The Inward Guide enables us to make contact with what we share most deeply with each other and with the whole of life. It is what unites us, what draws us into community and leads us to overcome

11

divisions in the human family; to be agents of reconciliation and mutual understanding. The leadings of the Guide will differ for each person, depending on their particular gifts and opportunities. As the Inward Light is filtered through our unique histories and abilities, it gives rise to ways of life that will often look very different. There are Quakers whose faithfulness to the leadings of the Spirit has led to them into befriending prisoners and refugees, political campaigning, teaching and caring for children, creating works of art, urban gardens and sustainable businesses, or to lives of prayer and compassionate listening. The Quaker tradition claims that through each of us following our own leadings, our individual gifts will complement and support each other, so that we can all make our own unique and irreplaceable contribution to the world.

The Quaker way helps us to cultivate habits of attention to the inward 'promptings of love and truth'; learning to recognise and cherish them, however small and inconsequential they may appear at first. This is how we develop the capacity to follow more challenging leadings if they arise. Through the regular discipline of listening to inward guidance in daily life we are gradually prepared for faithfulness in more demanding ways.

In Quaker experience it is rare for the full implications of a leading to be revealed before we take any practical steps to begin putting it into action. Rather than illuminating the whole of our future way, the Inward Light is far more likely to reveal obscure hints and mysterious attractions or resistances. Most commonly a leading will make itself known as an inner prompting to a particular course of action, or a feeling of being drawn towards a particular place or people, without any clear idea of the ultimate outcome.

It is through acting on these obscure leadings that we meet with the experiences that make us capable of receiving further insight. We gradually learn to trust our Guide by repeated practice. By trusting in the guidance we have received and taking the first step to respond, the next step becomes clear. This is a process of inner surrender, of gradual growth in trust and the abandonment of our fierce, anxious hold on autonomy; a patient dissolving of our inner defences to become more attentive, sensitive and receptive to the divine light within. Only when we look back over the course we have followed, might we eventually perceive how we have been guided, accompanied and supported to fulfil the leadings of the Spirit for our lives.

Quakers have traditionally taken great care to avoid going beyond the specific guidance the Spirit has shown them. This scrupulous attention to 'staying close to the Guide' reflects the experience that inward leadings are often frustratingly partial and piecemeal. There can be a great temptation to escape uncertainty and discomfort by rushing forward to embrace a new plan or to abandon a commitment that has become uncomfortable. This is the danger that Quakers have described as 'outrunning the Guide'; substituting our own need for certainty and control in place of openness and dependence on the living activity of God's Spirit within us.

Living through a period of attentive waiting, unknowing, and patient inward change is an essential preparation for Spirit-led action. This is what eventually enables us to recognise the path to which we are called by God, and to distinguish it from short-lived enthusiasms or self-interested motivations. Quakers are usually cautious about allowing themselves to be swept into hasty decisions by passionate enthusiasm or emotional appeals. Their alternative is not reliance on calculating reason or abstract principle, but waiting for a more subtle sense of 'rightness'; a quiet inner conviction that may have little to do with emotional excitement or calculation:

A few steps taken in the life and power of God are much safer and sweeter than a hasty progress in the hasty, forward spirit. (Isaac Penington, 1661)

Meetings for Clearness

When Quakers encounter a leading that could result in a major commitment, or when facing a potentially life-changing decision, they may ask their community for support with their discernment through a 'Meeting for Clearness'.

In early 2010 I came across an advert for the post of Director at a Quaker vocational training centre in Zimbabwe. Kate and I had talked about working in Africa at some time in the future, probably when our children had left home, but at this point they were seven and eight years old. Zimbabwe had recently been through a total economic collapse and was still under the authoritarian rule of Robert Mugabe, so when I applied and was offered the job we faced a decision with potentially serious consequences.

As part of a Quaker community, we were able to draw upon the discernment of our meeting to help us, by using a Meeting for Clearness. This involved asking several Quaker friends whose judgement we respected to meet with us in our home. After a period of silent worship together, we explained the decision we had to make, and our reasons, feelings and motivations.

The group listened carefully, without offering advice or opinions, and gently asked us questions to draw out the motivations and concerns that had not been expressed; how it might affect the children's education or friendships, whether one of us was more enthusiastic or had more reservations than the other, how we had thought through the risks involved. The meeting was a resource for bringing to the surface our desires, doubts, hopes and anxieties, so that we could become clear about how the Inward Guide was leading us. Once the issues had been thoroughly explored, we felt clear that this was a step we were being led to take. The group did not make the decision for us, but it helped us to be reassured that we had tested our leading as carefully as possible.

Way Opening

There often seems to be a mysterious correspondence between the inward leadings of the Spirit and the apparent cooperation of outward events. Quakers of every generation have observed the extraordinary ways that circumstances have apparently conspired to make their leadings possible, even against all probability.

When Kate and I were living in Liverpool in the year 2000, the UK government started to disperse large numbers of newly-arrived asylum-seekers all over the country for the first time. Previously, asylum-seekers had been concentrated in London and the south-east of England, and there were relatively few in most northern towns and cities.

As asylum-seekers started to be sent to Liverpool, we felt led to help with welcoming them. We even discussed moving house (again) in order to be closer to the areas where they were being housed. Within a few months of that conversation, several hundred asylum-seeker families were moved into our immediate neighbourhood, and we began to get to know them as neighbours and friends. With some other local people, we were able to set up a drop-in centre in a church hall to welcome new arrivals. This eventually developed into the charity Asylum Link Merseyside, which is still supporting asylum-seekers and refugees in Liverpool over fifteen years later.

Among Quakers and others who follow the leadings of the Spirit, experiences such as this are surprisingly common. Early Quakers described this process as 'way opening', and saw it as a confirmation of the right discernment of a leading. Someone who discerned a leading to action might be advised to wait until 'way opens', which would indicate the right time to undertake it. A leading to a particular action – a voyage, a project or form of service, may be carefully weighed and considered, but finding the right time to act often relies on a combination of outward circumstances coming together to 'open a way' for it.

'Way opening' does not mean that everything will be easy, or that there will be no obstacles or uncertainties. Following a leading often involves perseverance and the willingness to confront challenges and opposition. As way opens, however, there will be offers of help and cooperation; a growing sense of shared commitment and support from others, despite the inevitable hardships or frustrations.

Unlike Quakers of previous generations, who confidently attributed such apparently miraculous happenings to the purposeful action of God in the world, modern Quakers do not share a single explanation for how inward leadings and outward events so often seem to conspire together. For some, it is seen as a manifestation of the will of God, as God acts both to reveal our divine calling and to open the way for us to be faithful to it. For others, this process of inner and outer correspondence may be understood as one aspect of a universe that is infused with spiritual energy, or simply accepted as mysteriously beyond human explanation.

The Christian Story

For all Quakers until recent times, their experiences of divine encounter, transformation and guidance were rooted firmly in the Christian story, and were expressed in the images and symbolic language of the Bible. The first generation of Quakers described their movement as 'Primitive Christianity revived'; a renewal of the authentic experience of the Christian Gospel that had been obscured and distorted by centuries of authoritarianism and collusion with social elites. Through their practice of collective waiting in the Light these Quakers felt that they had made direct contact with the same divine power that was in Jesus of Nazareth, which they called 'the Inward Christ'.

Early Quakers identified their experience of transformation by the Inward Light as a 'dying to self' and a resurrection to new life that echoed the story of the life of Jesus. They interpreted the Quaker movement as the historical fulfillment of the biblical promise of Christ's return, announcing that the time of dependence on outward teachers was over, because 'Christ has come to teach His people Himself'.

Although the great majority of Quakers worldwide remain strongly rooted in the Christian tradition, there are also significant communities of Quakers who understand their experience through a broad range of different stories and spiritual paths. As societies in large parts of the world have become increasingly religiously diverse over recent decades, Quaker communities have also incorporated spiritual ideas, imagery and language from many different traditions. Many Quakers in the UK, US and elsewhere now interpret their Quaker practice without reference to specifically Christian language, and some rely on the language and imagery of Buddhism, paganism or other alternative spiritualities alongside or instead of biblical imagery.

It has proved possible to sustain Quaker communities with an unusual diversity of religious ideas because of the centrality of shared practice, rather than statements of belief, for the Quaker way.

From the beginnings of their movement, Quakers have recognised the inadequacy of all attempts to define faith in specific forms of words. In modern times, this has led many Quakers to see all language as inadequate to fully capture or describe the spiritual reality that can only be known by personal experience. The many different stories and forms of language that are used by Quakers today are recognised as always imperfect, but potentially complementary, approaches to the experience of encounter with a spiritual reality that is greater and more mysterious than any of our ideas about it.

In western cultures, it has been assumed for centuries that beliefs are the essence of religion. Differences of belief have been a cause or a pretext for horrific wars and persecutions. Taking our own beliefs as the only truth of reality, whether religious or secular, has led to continuous attempts to impose them on others. This is despite the apparent evidence that all claims to knowledge of spiritual reality are unprovable, and no doctrine or interpretation can ever decisively demonstrate its exclusive truth. It would appear instead that all religious beliefs are partial, revealing different faces of reality according to our different cultures, temperaments and life experiences.

Recognising the value of differing religious stories is not a denial of the truth that they seek to describe. It simply means acknowledging that there is more than one valid way to describe spiritual reality. Different religious beliefs, even apparently contradictory ones, can express contrasting aspects of a divine reality that is incomparably larger and deeper than any of our stories about it. The mainstream Christian tradition has tended to identify the doctrines of the various churches with divine Truth. It has often been claimed that there is only one true understanding of God, one correct interpretation of the Bible, and one authentic set of concepts, images and symbols for expressing the truth of God. By contrast, many Quakers today recognise a multiplicity of languages, symbols and concepts as potentially helpful, but always partial, pointers towards the mystery of divine activity in the world.

The Quaker tradition claims that purely intellectual assent to any doctrine or belief is irrelevant to our real spiritual needs and calling. For Quakers, it is not 'belief' in abstract doctrines that is important, but 'faith'; the attitude of trusting with one's whole self in the guidance of the Spirit within. To experience this Inward Guide at work in our lives and to trust ourselves to its healing and transforming power it is not necessary to accept any particular set of beliefs. This is the sense in which Quakers since the seventeenth century have recognised that what they called the Spirit of Christ is the same power at work in the people of every religion and none who are responsive to the divine Light within.

The humble, meek, merciful, just, pious, and devout souls are everywhere of one religion; and when death has taken off the mask they will know one another, though the divers liveries they wear here makes them strangers.
(William Penn, 1693)

For Quakers, it is the experience of encounter with the Spirit, rather than any intellectual belief, that is essential for connection to the divine purposes and each other. It is our relationship with a profoundly mysterious dimension of reality, beyond the power of our intention to fully name or understand, that summons us beyond ourselves to lives of self-giving, healing and peacemaking. The Quaker response to divine guidance is in action rather than theory. Any insights we may receive into God's nature and purposes are not given to bolster our own sense of certainty or identity, but for putting into practice, for making our own contribution to the healing and reconciliation of the world.

Chapter 3

Life in Community

Our life is love, and peace, and tenderness; and bearing one
with another, and forgiving one another, and not laying
accusations one against another; but praying one for another,
and helping one another up with a tender hand.
(Isaac Penington, 1667)

Those of us who are drawn to explore a religious tradition are
often looking for the experience of community. For some, it is in
times of hardship or challenge, such as new parenthood, divorce
or bereavement, that they discover the need for a wider circle of
supportive relationships. A local religious community may offer
the kind of intergenerational practical and emotional support
that is often missing in modern lifestyles.

When we moved to Sheffield with two pre-school children,
we were very grateful to find a Quaker community that included
several other young families. As our children have grown up
among Quakers they have benefited from a wide circle of other
children and adults, who have befriended and mentored them
in various ways. Members of our Quaker Meeting share their
lives with each other in large and small ways. We get together
for meals, to help with house moves and repairs, to assemble
furniture and share childcare, holidays and days out.

It is experiences such as these that many people are looking
for in a religious community; but just because communities are so
valuable, they can also be places of bitter disappointment when
they fail to live up to our expectations. Actual communities are
always more complex and ambivalent than our ideals, because
they are composed of real people with all their infuriating
contradictions. Every community has its share of disagreements,

personality clashes, irritations and resentments, which are elements of all human relationships. Like all other organisations, religious communities also have to find ways to deal with perennial dilemmas of power, authority and responsibility. The ways that different religious traditions cope with the challenges of social organisation have important consequences for the health of their communities. Many of the hurts and injustices suffered by members of religious groups are caused by inherent problems in their structures of authority and decision-making.

Some religious and secular movements aspire to be 'leaderless groups', organised on a basis of complete equality and governed by consensus; but such groups are particularly vulnerable to what feminist writers have identified as 'the tyranny of structurelessness'. Because there are no explicit leadership roles with identifiable limits to their authority, a few charismatic individuals can dominate decision-making, and vulnerable people are easily isolated and scapegoated. This pattern has been repeated regularly in the women's, environmental and peace movements, as well as in many religious communities. It seems to be an inherent feature of human groups that power and leadership will always emerge, whether acknowledged or not.

Historically, most forms of religious community have been organised hierarchically, with a separate class of religious leaders who make the decisions for the whole group. The leaders of these communities are often able to avoid most overt conflict by imposing a decision that is (at least in theory) in the interests of the community as a whole. At its best, where leaders exercise authority with sensitivity to people's needs, this provides a clear structure for decision-making, in which responsibility and accountability are explicit and visible. Official leadership roles usually have defined limits, and there are often procedures for appealing the decisions of those in authority. In such a community, leaders have the opportunity to listen to the needs and views of the whole group, and to defend the interests of vulnerable minorities or those who might otherwise be overlooked.

This model of community organisation has enabled the survival of diverse religious communities for thousands of years, including Christian and Buddhist monasteries and the Roman Catholic and Orthodox Churches. In the early 2000s I lived for a while in a lay community attached to a Catholic monastery, which was governed according to the 1500-year-old Rule of St Benedict. The monastery was governed by an Abbot, elected every eight years by all the fully-professed monks and given complete authority over the material and spiritual well-being of the community. As one of the monks explained to me, the Abbot even had the right to redistribute any of the community members' possessions. 'But,' he added, 'I'd like to see him try.' Despite his theoretically dictatorial power, as a member of a relatively small community the Abbot had a very strong motivation to listen carefully to everyone's views and to consider their needs. After all, he would have to carry on living with them for the rest of his life.

The drawbacks of hierarchical decision-making are, of course, well known. It is easily subverted by those in authority to serve their own interests at others' expense. Leaders are able to make decisions that benefit themselves, or simply reflect their own partial views and experiences, instead of representing the needs and interests of other community members. It is also common for hierarchical religious groups to discriminate against women and minorities, especially those who don't conform to approved sexual identities. Access to this authority has often been limited to men, and (at least in theory) heterosexuals. Through setting up inherently unequal relationships, hierarchies also facilitate sexual, emotional and financial exploitation. Such abuses have been a recurring feature, not just of well-publicised Roman Catholic institutions, but also of some large western Buddhist groups and other communities in which power is monopolised by charismatic spiritual teachers.

A common remedy for these failings is to introduce more democracy into community governance. Churches and other religious groups that are run on a democratic model benefit from greater legitimacy and equality of relationships. They also encourage more active participation by their whole membership. Unfortunately, the voting system has a built-in tendency to polarise views, which tends to turn decision-making into a competition with winners and losers. In a democratic vote, even a very small majority can claim total victory over the other side, and proceed to ignore the losers' views and interests entirely. This inevitably tends to create dissatisfied losing minorities, who have no commitment to the decision that has been made, and are likely to feel that their views have been ignored.

Many of the problems of religious communities are inevitable features of every organised social group. In any community there will be informal hierarchies of power and influence. Some members will be better informed, better connected, more charismatic or well-regarded than others. Even in the most democratic community, many people will prefer to be passive consumers of services provided by others, rather than taking a share of responsibility for shaping them. People's circumstances and capacities also differ, so that those with personal confidence, professional expertise and free time are much more likely to be available to perform the work necessary for running community organisations. Those who do engage in decision-making processes may be unrepresentative of the wider community, and their own views and priorities may come to predominate over others.

All of these tendencies can contribute to disillusionment with religious communities, especially by those who have felt hurt, marginalised or unfairly treated. Some religious teachings can intensify this disappointment by a utopian optimism, which claims that community should be a place without disagreement and conflict. An excessive emphasis on ideals of harmony tends to pathologise normal disagreements, and often pressures members into a compulsory conformity.

Deep human needs for both freedom and belonging are not easily reconciled. In some religious groups, strong bonds of mutual support come at the cost of obligatory obedience to the group's requirements of belief and behaviour. Members of these groups face the explicit or implied threat of being 'shunned' or excluded if they fail to conform. The threat of losing precious community relationships can inflict intense psychological and social pressure on individuals, while enhancing the power of the leadership to control their behaviour.

Quaker Community

Differences in views and interests are unavoidable in any group or community. Diverse temperaments and experiences create different preferences, and every group has to prioritise the use of limited resources. The challenge for healthy religious communities is to enable strong bonds of mutual support without imposing conformity, through practices that enable authority and decision-making to be transparent, accountable and open to everyone. Quaker communities attempt to do this through a unique practice of self-governance, in which every member of the community has an equal say in decision-making. Perhaps surprisingly, this form of organisation has endured for over 360 years, through huge social and cultural changes, without resorting to either majority voting or hierarchical leadership.

In a Quaker community the authority to make decisions is not held by a separate leadership group, but by all members of the community. Communities appoint some members to hold responsibility for particular areas of work for a limited time, such as finances or spiritual and pastoral care, and often set up committees or sub-groups to take care of essential tasks. But these groups and individuals are accountable to the meeting of the whole community, which delegates authority for limited purposes and periods, but retains the final say in all decision-making.

Quaker decision-making is carried out through a regular practice of collective discernment, which is essentially a Meeting for Worship with a focus on the particular issues requiring communal discernment and action at the time. All members of the community can participate in this 'Meeting for Worship for Business', to discern the leadings of the Spirit for the guidance of the community as a whole. This practice aims to draw on the insights and perspectives of everyone present to perceive the Spirit's guidance for the community at that particular time.

This practice of spiritual discernment relies on a shared trust that there is a reliable source of guidance and authority to be found, that is not simply a projection of our own wishes and values. Discernment is the practice of insight into a depth of reality that we can trust to guide us, and that is wider and deeper than whatever attitudes and values we bring individually or collectively to the occasion.

Over centuries, Quakers have found that the capacity for discernment is not restricted to a few people with special insight or advanced training, but is potentially available to the whole community. The Spirit can, and does, speak through even the least confident or experienced person. Their non-hierarchical forms of organisation and decision-making are grounded in this historical experience.

The decision-making authority for issues affecting the whole Quaker community in Britain rests with an annual Meeting for Worship for Business, to which all British Quakers are invited to participate. In this meeting too, everyone is entitled to contribute their insights on a basis of complete equality, whatever their age, sex or background. The Quaker tradition makes the ambitious claim that a community can conduct all of its decision-making, in large and small matters, as an attempt to perceive and follow the leadings of the Spirit, but no claim is made for its infallibility. Despite our best efforts, our discernment will always be incomplete and open to correction or improvement. All Quaker discernment is provisional and open to future change, because they recognise that all attempts to describe or understand God's purposes for themselves and the world are always partial and limited, in need of continual openness to fuller understanding. This rules out the kind of dogmatic certainty that has caused some religious groups to try to impose their definition of God's will on others by force or manipulation. Quaker commitments and insights are often held to with great firmness and determination, as the most reliable perception of reality that a community has available so far. But they are also open to the possibility of change as a result of new insights in the future, so that one of the most cherished pieces of Quaker advice is the encouragement to 'think it possible you may be mistaken'.

Of course, most collective decision-making in Quaker communities is concerned with relatively mundane matters of finances, social events, children's activities or managing premises. These issues rarely have an obvious connection with spiritual discernment, but the regular practice of Meeting for Worship for Business in routine matters helps to develop the community's capacity to discern more far-reaching issues. The discipline of a Meeting for Worship for Business requires everyone to put aside preconceived intentions about the best outcome; to open themselves to other perceptions, experiences and suggestions. There is no place for forceful argumentation, and each point of view or suggestion is listened to carefully, with a pause between each speaker. Participants also try to avoid repeating points that have already made by others, because the aim is to discover the different perspectives that the community has to offer on the question before them, and to consider them all in a tender and discerning spirit.

When everyone has had an opportunity to speak, the

meeting's clerk tries to record how the community has come to see this issue in a written minute. The minute is read out, and will either be accepted by the whole meeting, or require revision or further discussion. Where there is no clear sense of agreement, a decision may be deferred to a future meeting for further discernment. Sometimes a situation of 'stuckness' will cause those who are divided to reconsider in the light of others' perspectives. Surprisingly often, this will result in some new suggestion, which is not the victory of one side over another, or even a compromise between opposing opinions, but a new and creative approach that no one present had thought of beforehand.

Because voting is not used, a majority cannot simply impose its will on those with an alternative view, so all participants have an obligation to try to find solutions that can be accepted by everyone in the community. This inevitably sometimes makes Quaker decision-making slower than more familiar democratic or hierarchical approaches, but it also avoids some of their most serious drawbacks.

By contrast with hierarchical organisations, all members of a Quaker community are challenged to participate in decision-making. Where everyone is encouraged to take part, they have to accept their own responsibility for contributing to discernment in helpful ways, including in the inevitable difficult situations that they might rather avoid. Unlike democratic voting systems, Quaker discernment avoids the creation of resentful losing minorities. Where there are significant differences of perspective, a solution has to be found that can be broadly accepted by the community as a whole. A majority view cannot sweep all opposition aside through numerical superiority.

The Quaker approach to collective discernment is sometimes described as a form of 'consensus decision-making', but it differs from most secular practices for group consensus in important ways. Firstly, the aim of a Meeting for Worship for Business is not simply to make a decision that is agreeable to everyone. As a form of discernment, it is an attempt to arrive at a decision that is guided by the leadings of the Spirit, even where that may be challenging or uncomfortable. Simply negotiating a compromise between two opposed viewpoints is not sufficient, since the aim is not to satisfy the participants but to be faithful to the Spirit's leadings in that situation.

Secondly, there is no straightforward individual right to veto a group decision, which could otherwise hold the group hostage to one person's stubbornly-held opposition. Although deeply-felt reservations to group discernment will be carefully considered, and may often lead the community to reconsider, the meeting can reach a decision even without complete unanimity. In practice, this is a very rare occurrence. Even when a community comes to a decision without total agreement, it keeps open the possibility that a minority voice, or even a lone dissenter, may turn out to be right, or to be expressing some important aspect of the truth that the community needs to keep in mind.

The regular practice of these disciplines helps to shape the character of people who engage in them, and the culture of the communities in which they are practised. People who participate regularly in Quaker decision-making are continually reminded of the necessity of listening to others who have different views and experiences. They become used to not trying to force through their opinions, and instead working to find decisions that incorporate the insights of everyone involved. They have to practise these difficult skills over and over again, and gradually become skilled at recognising the wisdom of others and the shortcomings and limitations of their own perspectives.

The first time I took part in a Quaker Meeting for Worship for Business I was impressed by the striking difference from decision-making I had experienced in other groups. The Quakers in that meeting showed a robust sense of personal responsibility, noticeably free from either deference or aggressiveness. They combined a confidence in their own authority with a willingness to listen and weigh the opinions of others. As a friend once described a roomful of Quakers in a Meeting for Worship for Business, 'they looked like a group of very thoughtful, reasonable people ... who must on no account be messed with'.

Welcoming Difference

The Quaker way of collective decision-making means that diverse backgrounds, experiences and views are all essential to good discernment. A Quaker community does not require conformity of beliefs or backgrounds because it does not need to fear or suppress difference of opinion. For Quakers, 'inspiration operating through diversity is God's way of working' (Ashworth & Wildwood, 2009). Difference can be welcomed, because it is integral to the way that Quakers seek communal guidance.

Quaker discernment relies on a range of viewpoints and experiences being made available to the community through the contributions of its members. None of us individually has the breadth of perspective to be able to see every side of a complex issue impartially, or to fully appreciate ideas that are very far from our own experience. In a community of people with diverse life journeys, we have the opportunity to learn from each other how to see and appreciate the world from many different points of view. It is this capacity to listen and learn from our differences that enables communities sometimes to get beyond partial or self-interested motives, and to recognise the divine 'promptings of love and truth', wherever they might be leading us. In practice, most Quaker communities fall short of the degree of social, ethnic and age diversity that we need to gain the fullest range of perspectives and experiences. Wherever a wider range of experience is available, our discernment is enriched and our communities are stronger, more faithful to the Spirit and full of life.

The practice of corporate discernment depends on enabling differences of opinion to come to the surface, revealing and weighing sometimes deeply felt disagreements. Conflict is sometimes essential within every community. If we try to avoid or eliminate it altogether, our discernment and decision-making will suffer, because we will miss out on some of the views and experiences that we need to hear. As Margaret Heathfield wrote in her 1994 Swarthmore Lecture:

> If we make it all too smooth and slick, if we do not allow conflict to emerge, we are not really practising our Quaker business method. To maintain a worshipping stance and yet to tolerate conflict is quite a challenge, but the search for Truth may require both. Two equally valid aspects of the Truth may be being put forward, and it may require some conflict, effort and time to reach towards the over-riding Truth which contains them both.

Conflict avoidance often leads to unresolved resentments and erosion of trust. The fear of confrontation may also prevent people from challenging disruptive or domineering behaviour, allowing the most opinionated or aggressive individuals to dominate a group. Instead of trying to avoid or ignore conflict, we need to develop the skills and confidence to respond to it in healthy and helpful ways.

For most of us conflict is deeply uncomfortable, but it is both inevitable and necessary in any relationship and any genuine community. The successful resolution of conflict depends on a refusal to resort to violence or dehumanising language, and a willingness to listen carefully to the real needs of the other. It also requires the courage to speak up when something is wrong, to express our own needs clearly and honestly, and to refuse co-operation with unjust situations. These are skills that can be learned, even in primary school, such as a Quaker-inspired project in Sheffield that teaches school pupils to become conflict mediators among their peer groups. I have been deeply impressed by the skillfulness and maturity with which children as young as ten have learned to practise conflict resolution; listening impartially to both sides, and encouraging disputants to find their own solutions, rather than relying on adult judgements or punishments.

Quaker Testimony

The Quaker community is not primarily concerned with its own well-being or with recruiting new members. It exists to serve the purposes of God in the world. The Quaker way is a tradition of practice, which can only be shared with others through the power of action and example. This is what Quakers have traditionally called their 'testimony'.

Throughout Quaker history, individual Friends have discovered leadings to act in ways that witness to God's purposes. These leadings have often started from a fresh perception of some social or political reality that reveals human opposition to God's purposes for the world. Early Quakers recognised the 'persecuting spirit' behind the harassment of religious minorities, and the 'spirit of oppression' made visible in the taken-for-granted institutions of slavery. They were led to oppose all forms of persecution, to reject social divisions of rank and status, and to refuse to participate in war or violence.

Leadings of the Spirit are given to individuals, but they are not simply 'personal truths' with no relevance for anyone else. Leadings that emerge with individual Friends about a situation of disharmony, injustice or oppression can challenge the whole community to discern the true nature of their society and its institutions. They offer an insight into the nature of reality and a call to enact the healing and transforming power of the Spirit; to be a vehicle for the reconciling action of God in the world.

As we practise collective discernment of the Spirit's leadings, 'we are all being tested together', according to the contemporary Quaker Marion McNaughton. The community

31

supports and challenges individuals to examine the origins of their leadings, to test whether they originate from the Spirit or from unacknowledged personal motives. At the same time, individual leadings challenge the whole community to reflect on its faithfulness to the promptings of the Spirit, and how it is being called to respond to this new insight.

Over time, this process of collective discernment has resulted in the development of the Quaker community's corporate testimony. 'Testimony' refers to ways of living and acting that embody Quakers' recognition of the divine purpose for their own community, and their witness to the rest of the world. This testimony has evolved over several centuries to include a wide range of commitments, such as opposition to war and the arms trade, supporting prisoners, solidarity with refugees and working to become a 'low carbon, sustainable community', among many other forms of life and witness.

Through a developing process of reflection, Quaker testimony continues to be revised and adapted in response to changing conditions and sensitivities. Just as some historical forms of testimony, such as distinctive forms of dress and speech, have been abandoned or modified over time, current commitments will continue to be tested and revised in future.

Quakers are not all actively involved in every expression of collective testimony. Each person has their own leadings, according to their particular circumstances and abilities. But among committed Quakers there is a shared recognition of the discernment of the whole community that is expressed in its collective testimony. Quakers generally respect corporate commitments such as opposition to war or rejection of gambling, although anyone might be led to challenge the discernment of the community in the light of new conditions or insights. There is a creative tension between individual and collective discernment, which is neither a blind conformity to group dictates, nor arbitrary individual preferences. It is a continuous conversation between the insights of individual Friends and the shared and inherited wisdom of the whole Quaker community.

Chapter 4

The Broken Life

Art thou in the Darkness? Mind it not, for if thou dost it will fill thee more, but stand still and act not, and wait in patience till Light arises out of Darkness to lead thee.
(James Nayler, 1659)

The religious path is often presented as a way to achieve inner peace and happiness, and to avoid suffering. Much popular spirituality claims that life is meant to be filled with peace and contentment; that pain and anguish are problems that can be overcome by the right attitude or technique. The promise of perfect contentment is seductive, but it can never be fulfilled, because it is based on the illusion that suffering is a mistake.

Suffering, ageing, sickness and loss are not regrettable failures to realise our true nature. They are inherent in the nature of embodied human life and our often-incompatible needs and desires. Any spirituality, therapy or ideology that promises an escape from these limitations neglects the truth that suffering is an essential dimension of human life. Growth in spiritual maturity does not mean escaping or transcending these experiences, but becoming more able to accept and learn from them; to receive the painful gifts that they have to offer.

The Quaker way, with its emphasis on the Inward Light, is sometimes mistaken for one of these otherworldly spiritualities. But Quaker experience includes a far more realistic appreciation of the role of suffering in human life. In modern culture it is generally taken for granted that the aim of life is 'happiness' (understood as a positive mood or pleasant emotional states) and that our choices should be based on deciding what will bring the most happiness and the least suffering. This is in stark contrast to the actions of those Quakers throughout history who have deliberately chosen persecution, impoverishment, and costly and dangerous commitments in response to the leadings of the Inward Guide. If their goal was happiness, Quakers would never have stood up to governments and oppressive church institutions to demand religious freedom. They would not have gone to prison for conscientious objection to conscription, or like the US Quaker Tom Fox, been murdered working for peace in Iraq. For the Quaker way, it is not happiness or freedom from suffering that is the goal of life, but faithfulness to the life of the Spirit within, whatever it brings.

Why should anyone choose to follow such a path, if it does not promise to give us happiness or spare us pain? Perhaps one answer is that there is a deeper need; for a life that is charged with meaning through relationship with the Inward Guide. Happiness cannot provide a meaning for life, because it depends on finding a meaning in something else. Pleasure, comfort and luxury rapidly give way to boredom and restlessness. Our deepest need is for a sense of the meaningfulness of our life. We can tolerate endless hardships and frustrations in enthusiastic service of a goal that is full of meaning for us. Without meaning, all our pleasures turn to ashes, and no rewards are sufficient to motivate us to action.

Quakers and others have been willing to endure persecution and hardship in the service of the Inward Guide, because its leadings are charged with meaning and purpose. The guidance of the Spirit has illuminated their lives with profound significance that made sacrifices worthwhile and brought the possibility of joy in the midst of suffering. The Quaker philosopher John Macmurray has described this understanding of the religious path:

When religion is real, it throws the centre of our interest and our action right outside ourselves. It is not about myself at all, or only incidentally and for a purpose that is not my own. It is about the world I live in and the part that I must play in it. It is not to serve my need but the need of the world through me. Real religion is not something that you possess but rather a power that lays hold of you and uses you in service of a will that is greater than your own.

Self-Perfection

Many people are attracted to a spiritual path by the desire to perfect themselves; to escape everything that is messy and unsatisfactory about their lives and become wholly good. The goal of perfection has been emphasised by many religious traditions, and it has a powerful appeal for those who feel an inward calling to change their lives and become a better person. But the ideal of perfection also has a shadow side. It can be tempting to contemplate our efforts at self-improvement and using them to construct a flattering picture of ourselves. Especially if we have felt inadequate or unacceptable in the past, it may be appealing to cast ourselves as a 'good person', and to defend that identity at all costs. In reality, all of us have our selfish impulses, resentments and hard-heartedness. The more heavily we are invested in maintaining an exaggerated view of our own goodness, the less likely we are to acknowledge the reality of those feelings. Instead, we may be tempted to deny our own faults, and to blame our conflicts or frustrations on others.

Those who come to believe that they are more ethically pure or spiritually advanced than others are tempted to rely on this supposed superiority as the basis of their identity. This requires others to be in the wrong, which inevitably leads to scapegoating of other people or groups who are labelled as morally inferior. If I know that I am a good person, then it must be the other's fault when we come into conflict. If my group is in the right, we must be justified in however we are treating those others who do not measure up to our standards.

This does not mean that we should make no efforts to change our behaviour. We can always take opportunities to choose more responsible or compassionate actions. But perhaps our aims should be more modest than self-perfection. We can choose to act more often with greater awareness, kindness or courage, without the illusion that we can ever transform ourselves into someone who is entirely free from any troubling qualities. Instead, we might adopt the more modest resolution to pay closer attention to our own motives, to the needs and feelings of others, and the subtle promptings of love and truth in our hearts and minds.

It is true that profound changes do take place in some people's lives. Some turn away from a life of purely selfish ends, and devote themselves to the care or service of others, or like George Fox, find themselves transformed by profound experiences that give them a new sense of conviction and purpose. Perhaps the most important sign of the authenticity of such apparent 'conversions' is that they are recognised and received as a gift. Profound changes in our capacities and motives are not earned by the application of deliberate techniques of self-improvement. They are received as the mysterious blessing of the inward principle of life, blossoming within us in its own time and according to its own rhythms.

A Second Adulthood

The life-giving activity of the Spirit cannot be hurried or manipulated at will. It has its own rhythms and cycles that continue throughout life, to which we need to be continually responsive. We will often be led in different ways, to develop different capacities, at different stages in our life. In youth, we usually need to develop self-confidence, responsibility and competence. For many of us the challenge of adulthood involves discovering a sense of identity, establishing ourselves in the world of work, perhaps finding a partner and creating a family. For some, this includes pursuing the ambition to make their mark on the world, to succeed in a career or to 'make a difference'. This may mean following a sense of calling towards some form of service to the world or our immediate community.

Later in life there arrives the invitation to a second passage that is less well-charted. We approach this when we begin to recognise that the future is no longer open to endless possibilities. It is too late to have chosen a different direction, lived a different life and become a different person. We realise that we will now never achieve most of our early ambitions; that even our successes turned out not to bring the kind of fulfilment we had expected. This is the beginning of the transition to what is sometimes known as a 'second adulthood'.

At this point, we might attempt to fight against the failure of our hopes by redoubling our efforts to become more successful, or by searching for a different, more satisfactory partner. On the verge of the second adulthood, all the life that we have left unlived clamours for our attention. We may be tempted to fight against it by clinging tightly to the same strategies and ideals that have guided us so far, when life is asking of us something very different.

This stage of life brings many people to a new stage of spiritual searching; disillusioned with their former identities and on a journey of inward discovery. For some, it is a path out of some form of fundamentalism, whether religious or secular, that has occupied all their energies and provided a strong sense of purpose for their adult life so far.

Dogmatic thinking represents a strong temptation for many people in the first half of life, as they struggle to forge a sense of self and to find a way of making a mark on the world. Fundamentalist religious beliefs, political ideologies or dogmatic rationalism all demand that we exclude parts of our experience from awareness. They require us to be righteous and right-thinking, to deny everything in us that is mysterious and subversive, and all the ways that the world fails to match up to the creed's authorised narrative. The longer we try to live up to these demands, the more unacknowledged experience we accumulate, and the greater the effort needed to defend an increasingly fragile world view. Eventually, if the weight of contradictory reality becomes too great to sustain, we face the collapse of our former certainties and the call to a new, more inclusive understanding of reality.

We are challenged to discover who we are when we find that we are not the person we tried to be. If we are patient and compassionate with ourselves, and are fortunate to have friends who can listen to everything in us that we find hard to acknowledge, we may come to accept our failings and darkness as indispensable to living on the far side of disillusionment.

The Quaker way offers a path of spiritual discovery that is opposed to all forms of ideological thinking. It is based on the practice of openness to reality; developing sensitivity and responsiveness to the subtle movements of the Inward Guide. The Quaker Meeting for Worship offers a practice for developing our awareness of what is, rather than insisting that reality conform to our ideas of what it should be.

The Quaker experience of guidance is not usually a discovery of perfect clarity, or the resolution of all doubt and uncertainty. Very often, the Inward Guide is encountered as an obscure series of 'nudges', which may be experienced as inner leadings towards some new area of activity or interest, without any clear goal or rational motivation. Or the Guide may make itself known in the form of a new and persistent discomfort with our current way of life; a dissatisfaction with ourselves that refuses to be ignored. This inner prompting towards change and growth is easily mistaken for a symptom of psychological disorder, especially where it is resisted or ignored and becomes increasingly insistent, so that it disrupts our habitual life. It can feel like depression, anxiety, or intense frustration, rather than the voice of the divine life within, urging us to something new.

At this point in our life it is common to receive an inward prompting to leave behind some outworn part of our identity, to re-examine our relationships, or to enter a new form of engagement with the world. It may happen that this leading towards new possibilities does not come all at once, in a blaze of inspiration and understanding. Instead, it may lead us into a prolonged passage of obscure uncertainty, in which we feel profoundly lost and confused, deprived of our usual landmarks and struggling to make sense of what is happening to us. It may be only much later, when the process of disintegration of old habits and assumptions has been completed, that we are able to recognise the purposefulness of the experience we have been through. This is the experience that early Friends described as 'the cross', identifying it with the 'crucifixion of our own will'; a dying to the old self and rebirth to a new life in closer relationship with the indwelling Spirit of Christ.

Sometimes the Guide makes itself known simply as an inner resistance to a new or familiar course of action. This is what former generations of Quakers described as 'a stop in their minds'. It can suddenly appear as an inward obstacle to a familiar way of living, which we have never previously had cause to question. The Guide might be making itself known in this way to alert us to a new need to reflect or change course. This new inner resistance might be bewildering, especially where there is no obvious reason for changing a course of action that seems otherwise reasonable or harmless. But it may be a sign of a new condition of inner restlessness; of something struggling to come to life in us, that is making us newly sensitive in areas of our life that no longer 'fit' with the person we are being called to become.

Sooner or later, for many of us, the new growth of life within, with its unexpected new sensitivities, will come into conflict with our settled habits of self-protection and self-interest. The journals of early Quakers often describe prolonged struggles against the new leadings and motives that are coming to life within them. In eighteenth-century New England, John Woolman wrestled with a growing awareness of the horrors of slavery at a time when many Quakers were slave-owners. Conscious of the inevitable conflict that would result from public opposition to slave-holding, he struggled with his leading to open the eyes of the Quaker community to the evil of slavery; both the suffering and oppression of people held as slaves, and the corruption of those who claimed ownership of them.

> Understanding that a large number of slaves had been imported from Africa into the town, and were then on sale by a member of our Society, my appetite failed; I grew outwardly weak ... I had many cogitations, and was sorely distressed.

Wrestling with the Angel

This inward struggle will be familiar to everyone who has ever been drawn towards some course that involves hardship, sacrifice, or simply the discomfort of the untried and unfamiliar. Most commonly, we try to evade the claims of the Inward Guide, and we are usually well-defended with arguments for avoiding change or risk. Our culture furnishes us with plenty of justifications for valuing security, comfort and self-interest over the discomforting leadings of the Spirit.

In the mysterious biblical story, Jacob is alone one night during a journey, when a man appears and wrestles with him until dawn. When Jacob refuses to let him go, the stranger dislocates Jacob's hip, but also gives him a blessing and a new name; 'Israel', which means 'struggles with God' (Genesis 32: 22–32).

This story is an image of the struggle with God that is crucial to the Quaker way. Early Quakers recorded that their initial encounter with the Inward Guide was often conflictual. The Light revealed aspects of themselves that they would rather not see, and urged them in directions they would rather avoid. As the leadings of the Inward Guide were resisted, the struggle would intensify, sometimes leading to severe physical illness or emotional crisis. Perhaps this kind of experience is so often glossed over today because many people are understandably suspicious of anything that suggests coercion or threat in religion. The biblical stories that portray God as threatening and punishing are usually rejected as outdated and unhelpful. But there is nevertheless an important reality of 'struggling with God' that takes place in our own experience, for many of us who have encountered the reality of the Inward Guide, but who have resisted what it has tried to show us and how it has tried to lead us.

This resistance can take many forms. We usually want to defend a favourable view of ourselves, and to ignore any inklings of our self-interested motives, resentments or narcissism. We are often reluctant to embrace nudges of the Spirit that suggest we might be led to disturb our habitual comforts in some way, by reaching out to unfamiliar people, or making some change in our daily life that involves risk or inconvenience. This kind of spiritual sluggishness or inertia is common to almost all of us, and perhaps acts as a necessary ballast to avoid being swept away by temporary enthusiasms. Unfortunately, it is all too easy to stay stuck in the defensive posture that insists on digging in, refusing to hear what the Spirit has to say to us, or to follow where it leads. All too often, the result is a life that goes nowhere, that continually circles around its collection of small concerns, and never breaks out of the track of narrow, habitual self-interest. It is perfectly possible to pass a whole lifetime in this way, in which the call of the Inward Guide is smothered so insistently that life withers away, and we are haunted by vague regrets and anxieties, crowded around by the insistent threat of meaninglessness.

For some of us, the rejection of the Light is more deliberate.

The dark impulses of addiction and compulsion, even when we recognise them and know them to be destructive, can draw us towards choices that we know to be harmful; self-harming through over-eating, alcohol, drugs or other compulsive behaviours. The deliberate impulse to self-destruction and extinction will be familiar to everyone who has struggled with addiction or despair. It is the urge to escape the agonising tensions, regrets, humiliations of life, by extinguishing feeling and responsibility. We can choose to fight against the Light, tearing at ourselves and wounding those around us in our furious rejection of inward life.

The experiences of early Quakers, like the story of Jacob, suggest that the struggle with God does not have to end like this. For some of us, the greatest blessing we ever receive might be a painful dislocation, when our life is interrupted by a suffering, failure or humiliation that knocks us out of our habitual self-justification and distractions. We might find that none of our goals are any longer worthwhile, that our cherished opinions or attitudes were meaningless posturing, and that we no longer know what to do or who to be. We have been brought to the point of surrender to the inward springs of life that were struggling to be born within us. Now we can receive a new name, a new identity and purpose for our life, because we have 'struggled with God' and thankfully, blessedly, we have been defeated.

Learning from Failure

The Quaker way is not a project of self-improvement, self-perfection or success. Modern culture encourages us to understand ourselves as a personality that can be managed and improved by the application of suitable techniques. Instead of this instrumental view of ourselves as 'things' to be optimised and manipulated, the Quaker way encourages an attitude of respectful attention to the profound processes of inward change and maturation that are at work within us throughout our lives, most often without our conscious intention or awareness.

This faith in the inward dynamic of our lives is part of the Quaker recognition of something sacred and mysterious in the depths of our experience. This divine activity, working below the level of our own intentions for our healing and reconciliation with all of life, is sometimes called 'the Seed'.

> Give over thine own willing, give over thy own running, give over thine own desiring to know or be anything and sink down to the seed which God sows in the heart, and let that grow in thee and be in thee and breathe in thee and act in thee; and thou shalt find by sweet experience that the Lord knows that and loves and owns that, and will lead it to the inheritance of Life, which is its portion.
>
> (Isaac Penington, 1661)

The Seed is a potent Quaker image for the life of the Spirit within us. It suggests both the fragility and smallness, as well as the awesome potential contained within the inner life. Like a seed, the inward life of the Spirit is not subject to our control or manipulation. Our responsibility is simply to provide the nurturing conditions that will enable it to flourish in its own time, according to its own inward pattern of development. We can choose to stifle the life of the Seed, by ignoring its needs for space and stillness, smothering it with distractions or destructive behaviour. We can also choose to shape our life so that it becomes a place where the Seed can develop and grow.

Each of us has the Seed of life within. If we allow it to, this seed will grow and unfold into a unique shape in our lives. The Seed takes its time to germinate and grow, it cannot be hurried. This demands patience and acceptance that the Seed contains its own inward dynamic, which may turn out to be quite different to the ideas or intentions we had for ourselves.

The growth of the Seed often seems to draw us into areas

of weakness and difficulty, into a confrontation with our limitations and anxieties. This is never a comfortable experience, but it may be essential for us to learn things that we need to know, to grow into to live the life we are called to. There is only so much that we can learn from success and achievement, which simply reinforce the behaviours and attitudes that seem to have paid off. Much of our learning has to come through experiences of failure and disappointment, when we are forced to reevaluate our habitual strategies, and to reassess our motivations and desires. When a relationship is in crisis, a career at a dead-end or a cherished project fails, there is a fresh opportunity to recognise what we have so far ignored or refused to acknowledge in ourselves and others. Most accounts of people's lives emphasise their achievements and successes. What may have been more significant is the many ways they have tried and failed, their griefs and losses, and the transformations in understanding and motivation that grew from failure.

When we returned from Zimbabwe in 2012, I had to struggle with my own experience of failure and disappointment. Despite all our efforts, it had proved impossible to make the training centre financially sustainable, without heavy job losses that it was politically impossible for me as a foreigner to impose. I had to accept the bitter reality of returning to the UK without having achieved what I set out to do. As someone who was very attached to an idea of my own competence, and reliant on others' high opinion of my abilities, it was a humiliation to have to confront my own limitations. Where I had become used to expecting my projects to succeed, I was forced to recognise that even my best efforts, in the service of a leading that seemed to be clearly from the Spirit, offered no guarantee of success. I found that I was no longer able to go back into the same kind of work I had done before. My energy and motivation for running charity projects had dried up. Instead, I ended up re-training in organic agriculture, and working for several years as a grower with a city farm.

We often seem to assume that life is like a map, with all of the routes laid out before us, so that we can choose our direction according to the destination we want to reach. This image takes for granted that we can see in advance all of the potential challenges and rewards, and be in charge of our own journey through our deliberate choices. For most of us, life only rarely conforms to our plans and intentions. Life is a dark wood: we cannot see what lies ahead, and all of our choices are made in ignorance. Unpredictable life-changing events wait for us around every corner. Serious illness, disability or mental anguish, the loss of a partner or child can strike at any time and utterly overturn all of our plans and intentions.

George Fox writes in his Journal of his early experience of profound confusion and 'temptation to despair':

> My body being as it were dried up with sorrows, griefs and troubles, which were so great upon me that I could have wished I had never been born ... I fasted much, and walked abroad in solitary places many days, and often took my Bible, and went and sat in hollow trees and lonesome places till night came on. And frequently in the night walked mournfully about by myself; for I was a man of sorrows in the times of the first workings of the Lord in me.

Later, he recognised how these times of severe trial had enabled him to 'know all conditions'; to understand the suffering and confusion of others, so that he could speak to their condition. The painful gift of extreme suffering, even as it seems to place us outside the normal experience of those around us, is the capacity to be alongside others who find themselves suddenly expelled from the complacent life of society.

Our shared vulnerability to unpredictable and helpless suffering is one of the things we all have in common. Its destructive power can shatter our defences against the world, creating a raw freshness of perception. People who have been through the torment of affliction no longer see the world in the same way. They can become acutely sensitised to the suffering of others, and disillusioned with the false promises, enticements and distractions of the surrounding culture. They have lost a protective layer of skin, and stand exposed to the raw currents of inhumanity, oppression and selfishness that swirl around them. Out of the dark night of this affliction, some receive the gift and summons to minister to their community, turning their new perception into insight that can bring healing to others.

For all of us, choosing to love, to care for other people and for the life of our world, means choosing to be vulnerable. The more connected we are, the more we are vulnerable to being hurt, to suffering with the other. This suffering is the cost of living a full human life, with all its weakness and uncertainty. The promise of a guided life is not avoiding these limitations, but becoming more able to embrace them, in order to bring into the world the unique gifts that we have to offer.

For those without obvious, visible woundedness or disabilities, it is always tempting to construct a persona of capability and strength, to deny their inner vulnerability in order to project an appearance of competence. There is an obvious appeal to concealing our own weakness and protecting ourselves from others. But it can become a dangerous burden when the pressure of life events makes it increasingly difficult to maintain a facade of invulnerability.

In a culture that expects and requires people to be only successful, healthy, competent and in control, where every sign of weakness or suffering is counted as a defect, there are overwhelming pressures to maintain a pretense of competence, even when it is sharply at odds with our inner reality. This can become an intolerable demand, which may lead to extreme acts of self-destructiveness. Actions that are dramatically out of character, apparently self-defeating or bizarre, may be ways that the reality of our life is rebelling against the impossible demands of our self-presentation. By crashing our life through reckless behaviour, we may be forcing ourselves to display our inner anguish or confusion, which couldn't find expression in the official face we have presented to the world. If, instead of denying our weakness and vulnerability, we are willing to acknowledge it to ourselves and others, perhaps we will be more able to avoid going to such destructive extremes.

We can choose to avoid feeling everything that is painful or frightening in our life. Overwork, distraction, alcohol, drugs and compulsive behaviour can insulate us from full awareness of the suffering that is part of being human. But the Quaker way is a path of choosing to be aware. Quaker practices bring us into intimate contact with all of the reality of our lives, including what is painful and humiliating. By choosing to recognise these aspects of ourselves we may avoid projecting our unacknowledged imperfections onto others. Without so much fearful judgement of others, we might also be less inclined to separate ourselves from people who remind us of the less acceptable parts of our own nature.

Choosing awareness means consenting to feel everything. We can try to shut ourselves off from experiencing what is going on in our hearts and minds, but we cannot blind ourselves only to what is undesirable or unpleasant. The refusal to be aware inevitably means losing contact with the whole range of experience; with joy and meaning as much as pain or despair. If we are ever to know the possibilities of a life that is rich in meaning, sooner or later we need to allow ourselves to feel, to see and to acknowledge it all. All of our experience is important, not just the parts that we want or intend. The promise of a guided life is not ease and comfort, it is the 'abundant life', that includes suffering and times of confusion, as well as meaning, purpose and joy.

Chapter 5

Choosing Life

Take heed, dear Friends, to the promptings of love and truth
in your hearts. Trust them as the leadings of God whose Light
shows us our darkness and brings us to new life.
(Advices & Queries 1)

Life in modern, liberal societies is unique in human history.
It offers an unprecedented space of freedom for personal
expression, exploration and self-creation. It also, sooner or later,
leaves many of us feeling anxious, lonely, and haunted by the
threat of meaninglessness.

Unlike traditional cultures, which provide a shared
framework of taken-for-granted values, liberal societies require
each of us to decide for ourselves what is meaningful and
valuable. In a radically diverse culture there are many options,
but no shared basis for making choices. We cannot help being
aware of so many contradictory viewpoints about what kinds
of goals are worthwhile that it may seem impossible to 'choose
how to choose'.

Modern values of individual freedom, autonomy and
independence are often pursued at the expense of other, equally
profound needs; for a sense of belonging, identity, the feeling of
being at home in a particular place with particular people. These
unmet human needs provide a powerful source of motivation
within a consumer economy. The entertainment and marketing
industries promise to fulfil deep needs for connection, status,
identity, transcendence and security through the purchase of
clothes, technology, holidays and insurance. These commodified
experiences and products hook into soul-needs that they can
never satisfy, creating a cycle of addiction that drives the endless

growth required by a capitalist economy.

Modern lifestyles keep many of us constantly on the edge of burnout; crowding in too many commitments, using food, alcohol and passive entertainment to stay afloat, and intensifying the pressures by overspending and denying ourselves time for deep rest or reflection. If we reach a point in our lives when we are drawn to explore a spiritual tradition we have received an invitation to 'wake up'. This often means becoming more aware of the dissatisfaction with how we are living, instead of smothering it with distractions. This can be a precious opportunity in our life; a time when we become open to the subtle nudges of the Spirit within, urging us to break out of our habitual routines into a fuller and a richer life.

Religious traditions at their best offer well-tested practices and healthy communities that help to nurture the life of the Spirit. They support ways of life that disclose the depth of meaning and beauty in the world, and that nourish the Seed of life within each of us. Over many generations, the Quaker tradition has developed ways of living that have enabled people to find a rich sense of their life's purpose, and to enrich and sustain the life of the world, without manipulating them into conformity. Some of these practices might be especially helpful for people in modern societies, including those who are not Quakers, because they answer to deep human needs that are often ignored by the dominant patterns of modern life. Many of them are expressed in the brief passages of practical and spiritual reflection known as 'Advices and Queries' .

The Advices & Queries are prompts to personal reflection in the light of the experience of the wider Quaker community. This tradition provides a framework for ethical and spiritual discernment informed by collective Quaker insights, which can help us to focus on our own choices and motivations. The Advices & Queries encourage us to pay attention to areas of life that Quakers have found to be important for developing and sustaining a life in relationship with the Inward Guide. They describe ways that we can nurture the Seed of divine life within us, by providing the conditions that enable it to flourish and grow.

Stillness

Do you try to set aside times of quiet for openness to the Holy Spirit? All of us need to find a way into silence which allows us to deepen our awareness of the divine and to find the inward source of our strength. Seek to know an inward stillness, even amid the activities of daily life.
(Advices & Queries 3)

The Quaker way of life is rooted in the practice of stillness. The stillness of 'waiting in the Light' in worship gradually reveals a dimension of experience that seems to lie underneath our everyday consciousness; the powerful dynamic stillness at the heart of existence. This experience of divine stillness, of being held by a peaceful and sustaining Presence, is the foundation of all Quaker spirituality and witness. This experience of being held or 'immersed' in stillness has been described by the modern Quaker William Taber:

I once thought worship was something I do, but for many years now it has seemed as if worship is actually a state of consciousness which I enter, so that I am immersed into a living stream of reality which has always been present throughout all history.

Quakers over many generations have found ways to cultivate daily reminders of this underlying presence, to continually renew their contact with the divine stillness which is the source of life. This is the intention behind the common Quaker practice of a 'silent grace'; a few moments of shared silence at the beginning of mealtimes, which encourages us to reconnect with the 'still, small voice' of the Inward Guide. This refreshing stillness can also be encountered through our participation in the natural world, in art or music, or in the intimate, undefended presence of another person.

Many Quakers make a regular practice of silent prayer or meditation that helps them to sustain an inward stillness throughout the day. This continuous contact with the living stream of inward stillness is treasured as a source of strength, purpose and healing. For some, it can become what Bernard Canter has described as 'a wordless and endless sureness. Like the silence of two friends together. Like the silence of lovers'.

The quality of awareness is of particular importance for Quakers, whose spiritual practice is grounded in sensitivity to the Inward Light in their hearts and minds. This capacity for inward stillness and patient attention is especially difficult to maintain in modern lifestyles that are often overcrowded with commitments, deadlines and distraction. Email and social media can contribute to a constant feeling of information overload, a pressure to read and respond to ever-growing volumes of communication, and increased anxiety about how we are regarded by others.

The mental habits that are developed by the pressures and temptations of information technology can become a significant obstacle to encountering the power of divine stillness. If we find that our relationship with any technology is tending to undermine our capacity for awareness, it may be important to consider changing the ways that we make use of it. We can make the choice to use online communication in ways that serve our real needs for connection and understanding, without allowing it to dictate how we use our time, or undermine our ability for sustained attention. Having recognised this in my own life, I have established the discipline of a rest from online communication every Sunday. I find that having at least one day a week without checking emails or social media helps to weaken the restless mental habits of constantly seeking distraction.

Simplicity

Attend to what love requires of you, which may not be great busyness.
(Advices & Queries 28)

The expectation of 'great busyness' can be a destructive pressure in modern societies. As resources are cut and workplaces 'rationalised', many people's work lives have become increasingly demanding, and it can be difficult to avoid constant anxiety about deadlines and performance targets. The Quaker way invites us to lay down the inward compulsion to be always doing and active, to step aside from the hectic scramble for achievement.

Many Quakers have made deliberate choices to limit the scope of their working lives, careers and businesses, in order to give a greater priority to unhurried relationships or service to their communities. In the eighteenth century, John Woolman made the decision to give up a promising retail business in order to concentrate on his religious ministry. He wrote that:

My mind, through the power of truth, was in a good degree weaned from the desire of outward greatness, and I was learning to be content with real conveniences, that were not costly, so that a way of life free from much entanglement appeared best for me, though the income might be small. I had several offers of business that appeared profitable, but I did not see my way clear to accept of them, believing they would be attended with more outward care and cumber than was required of me to engage in. I saw that an humble man, with the blessing of the Lord, might live on a little, and that where the heart was set on greatness, success in business did not satisfy the craving; but that commonly with an increase of wealth the desire of wealth increased.

Many modern Quakers have made similar choices, accepting reduced incomes and more limited career prospects in order to give more time and energy to aspects of life that nourish their inner lives and relationships, and that are of service to others.

Quakers have traditionally adopted lives of comparative simplicity, as a way of reducing the pressure to maintain lifestyles of acquisition and excess. This is a countercultural attitude in a consumer culture that is based on accumulation and competitive consumption. Simplicity is not an expression of austerity or asceticism, but a natural outgrowth of the desire to keep life focussed on what brings vitality and significance; to avoid being burdened and harassed by the pursuit of possessions, income and status.

Try to live simply. A simple lifestyle freely chosen is a source of strength. Do not be persuaded into buying what you do not need or cannot afford.

(Advices & Queries 41)

The Quaker tradition of cultivating simplicity in daily life does not mean rejecting the sensual enjoyment and beauty of food, clothes, furniture or belongings. Generations of Quakers have found that by simplifying their lives and possessions they have come to a deeper appreciation of the richness and beauty of the physical world. We can be nourished by the beauty of our surroundings and the things we see and touch every day. Especially when many of us are forced to spend our working lives in environments that are bland or ugly, it is important for our homes and community spaces to embody a sense of beauty and hospitality.

The first time I was invited to a Quaker home I was struck by the practical simplicity of its furnishings; well-made wooden furniture, a hand-made quilt and beautiful crockery. Nothing in the house was disposable, shoddy or ostentatious. This is a distinctive kind of beauty that the psychotherapist Thomas Moore describes as 'the spiritual richness of simplicity':

> Simplicity doesn't mean meagreness but rather a certain kind of richness, the fullness that appears when we stop stuffing the world with things ... Let us feel the textures and see the colours, and then we won't need so many things in the place to make it nurturing.

Consumer culture treats all of physical reality as landfill in waiting. Most of our possessions are designed to become rapidly obsolete and thrown away rather than repaired and maintained. The richness of simplicity involves cultivating a greater appreciation for the things that surround us in our daily lives, a commitment to valuing and caring for them, instead of constantly discarding and replacing them with something new.

Forgiveness

> Do you foster the spirit of mutual understanding and forgiveness which our discipleship asks of us? Remember that each one of us is unique, precious, a child of God.
> (Advices & Queries 22)

In the practice of Quaker worship and discernment, we are challenged to 'stand still in the Light'. In place of our habitual strategies of preoccupied busyness, we are confronted with what is. For many of us, that eventually means having to sit with our brokenness, our weakness and our failures. As we grow into a clearer perception of our own habits of self-protection, of blaming, criticising or evasion of reality, it is easy to become discouraged by the gap between the person we intended to be, and the reality of our inevitable compromises and failings. The Quaker experience is that as our hurts and disappointments are gradually revealed by the Inward Light, we are accepted, healed and held by a divine Presence that does not condemn or reject any part of us.

If we can be patient with everything that is dark and troubling in ourselves, we will also be more understanding of others. We will no longer feel the necessity to blame or condemn those whose behaviour is selfish, destructive or manipulative, because we recognise the same potential within ourselves. Every person has disappointed themselves and others. Every one of us, once we are able to let go of the strident demands of self-justification, has a need for forgiveness. Seeing this in ourselves helps us to grow into the capacity to forgive others.

The capacity to understand and forgive is essential to resolving conflict in our daily lives. In our families, communities and workplaces conflicts and resentments often wear away at people because they are never resolved or reconciled. Each of us, through our everyday relationships, can contribute to bringing understanding and reconciliation to those around us. Instead of feeding resentment and blame, simply listening to others without judgement is a powerful source of peacemaking. By speaking truthfully and acting with kindness and integrity, people from every background are sources of continuous healing in their communities. This gift of everyday peacemaking is a fruit of inner faithfulness to the life of the Inward Guide, the Seed of insight and understanding.

The well-known Quaker commitment to peace is sometimes thought of as a pacifist ideological stance. It is truer to the roots of Quaker spirituality to see peacemaking as a natural outgrowth of the life of the Spirit, as it opens our eyes to our own darkness and kindles our commitment to healing injustice and division in the human family. The early Quakers explained their refusal to participate in war as a direct result of the activity of God within them, which had freed them from the selfish desires that led to violence:

> We know that wars and fightings proceed from the lusts of men (as Jas. iv. 1–3), out of which lusts the Lord hath redeemed us, and so out of the occasion of war ... All bloody principles and practices, we, as to our own particulars, do utterly deny, with all outward wars and strife and fightings with outward weapons, for any end or under any pretence whatsoever. And this is our testimony to the whole world.

Truthfulness

Are you honest and truthful in all you say and do?
(Advices & Queries 37)

Early Quakers went to great lengths to practise plain and truthful speech at all times and on all occasions. Truthfulness, honesty and integrity were testimonies to the renewed lives of people who felt themselves to be freed from the self-serving motives that required dishonesty and deception. Through their experience of inward liberation, they became able to commit themselves to a fearless singleness of purpose, without any desire for concealment or equivocation.

Complete truthfulness is usually considered both unrealistic and undesirable in contemporary culture. Most people consider 'white lies' essential to smooth over potential embarrassments. Truthfulness is certainly very difficult to practise in everyday social and work situations. It is important not to give unnecessary offence, and there are sometimes strong incentives to lie in order to avoid significant personal inconvenience. But the habit of reaching for the easy 'social lie' as a first resort evades the challenge to find a way of speaking honestly that is also tactful and considerate of others. A more truthful response will often require greater openness and vulnerability. It may mean exposing more of our real feelings, needs and values, instead of hiding behind conventional excuses.

Habits of truthfulness are important, not just for our own integrity, but principally for the building and maintenance of trust. Truthful speech and honest behaviour are essential conditions of relationships in which we can trust that someone will say what they mean, and do as they say. Without this background of social trust, we are condemned to live in a 'post-truth' world, in which we don't even expect people to speak honestly, or to take our own statements seriously. Instead, speech is regarded simply as an instrument for manipulating each other for our own purposes.

Lying may sometimes be necessary to prevent greater harm, especially by those in positions of political power or great responsibility. There may be an unavoidable clash between the demands of personal integrity and public responsibility. But the fact that deception is sometimes necessary does not mean that it is not in itself an evil, to be avoided wherever possible. The existence of some 'hard cases', where it is unclear how lying can be avoided without causing greater harm, does not make truthfulness irrelevant. On the contrary, it should emphasise the importance of cultivating habitual truthfulness in our daily life, in order to distinguish those occasions when lying may be unavoidable from when it is simply convenient.

The Quaker commitment to plain and truthful speech extends beyond simply avoiding lies. Quakers have traditionally taken care to avoid conforming to conventions of exaggeration, flattery, manipulation and games of status and one-upmanship. They have pointedly refused to use flattering titles for religious or secular leaders in order to emphasise their witness to the fundamental equality of all people.

The traditional Quaker practice of 'plain speech' involves a careful attention to the ways that we habitually communicate and their impact on all our relationships. It is a spiritual discipline that involves a growing sensitivity to the subtle motivations of our speech and online communication. It means developing our awareness of the consequences of our words on ourselves and others, and choosing to speak and write in ways that build up peaceful, healthy and truthful relationships.

Friendship

Seek to know one another in the things which are eternal, bear the burden of each other's failings and pray for one another. As we enter with tender sympathy into the joys and sorrows of each other's lives, ready to give help and to receive it, our meeting can be a channel for God's love and forgiveness. (Advices & Queries 18)

The Quaker way is not a solitary search for individual enlightenment; it is a way of friendship. We rely on each other for mutual support, encouragement, discernment and learning throughout our lives. Quakers are not self-sufficient spiritual seekers, but a community of friends who aim to discern the leadings of the Spirit, and act on them, together.

Many of the aims of Quaker practice are not just individual goals. Collective discernment, corporate testimony and supportive community are irreplaceable aspects of the Quaker way that can only be discovered together with others.

For people who are understandably wary of religious institutions, it can be difficult to accept the importance of being involved in a particular local community. The prospect of joining a distinct religious group can feel like a threat to our freedom and individuality. Like all other religious groups, Quaker communities have their own culture, history and traditions, but they do not rely on conformity. Newcomers to a Quaker community are not expected to sacrifice their individuality, their opinions, beliefs, identities or personal histories. Becoming part of a Quaker meeting is not a process of surrendering to a group's dictates and expectations. It is a mutual recognition of the same Spirit acting in our lives, and a commitment to sharing and learning from our differences, in order to more fully discover and reflect the breadth of the divine life in the world.

Quakers refer to each other as 'Friends', and friendship in all its aspects plays an important role in Quaker spirituality. A friend is not just someone whose company we enjoy, but one who values what is most important to us. A friend cares about our genuine well-being, and is willing to challenge as well as to affirm us in our efforts to realise it. Friendship enables us to know that we are not alone in the spiritual life, that others are struggling, learning, failing and persevering alongside us; drawn by a longing for connection with the same Inward Guide. We can help each other to develop this connection by our patience with each other, our care for one another, our honesty and openness about everything that is most precious and most difficult in our lives.

A local Quaker community creates possibilities of friendship with people of different generations and life journeys. This includes people whose differences of temperament or background make them difficult for us to be with, and unlikely candidates for personal friendship. Sharing the practices of Quaker worship and discernment together creates bonds of common interests and activity, even with people who might otherwise never know each other.

In societies and lifestyles that are often segregated by age and class, communities of people from diverse backgrounds enable us to spend time with those who are different to ourselves. This gives us an opportunity to learn from our differences, including about our own judgements and prejudices. We may become able to understand and appreciate unfamiliar people; to grow into the possibility of unlikely friendships.

I am continuously learning from Quakers in my community and from different parts of the world, often through the quality of their presence more than anything explicitly said. Some Quakers have taught me by the example of their lives, such as the Zimbabwean Richard Knottenbelt, who as a young man was imprisoned for refusing conscription into the Rhodesian army. Others have provided examples of wholehearted listening, hospitality and generosity that have influenced my own life, and strengthened my sense of gratitude and belonging.

These and many other Quaker friends feel like a kind of extended family, in many countries and reaching back through many generations. None of them are perfect. We all have our shortcomings and weaknesses, but by sharing our lives we are able to nourish the divine life in each other and in the world in ways that none of us could accomplish on our own.

Living Adventurously

Live adventurously. When choices arise, do you take the way that offers the fullest opportunity for the use of your gifts in the service of God and the community? Let your life speak. (Advices & Queries 27)

Our deepest need is for communion; intimate relationship with the presence of God within and between us. Through this relationship, we can encounter a source of healing for our wounds, and meaning and purpose for our lives. By allowing ourselves to trust in the guidance of the Inward Light, by accepting what it reveals to us and the direction in which it orients our lives, we enable the divine life to make use of our particular histories and abilities, with all of our inevitable contradictions. Embarking on this way means surrendering the anxious attempt to control the direction of our life, and consenting to be guided and shaped by the Spirit of life within us.

The guided life is not a way to become successful. While a few people might be led into lives of conspicuous achievement, for most of us the Inward Guide appears to have different priorities. Most people, whether Quakers or not, who allow their lives to be shaped and guided by the Spirit have relatively unremarkable careers and never occupy positions of national attention. Some are guided into lives of long-term faithfulness to a particular vocation or community; making, repairing, teaching, raising children, caring for sick or disabled loved ones or strangers. Others are led in different directions at different times over the course of their lives. But everyone who submits to the life-giving guidance of the Inward Light contributes something essential to the well-being, the beauty and the healing of the world. To consent to live a guided life means choosing to give ourselves, to share our gifts, take risks, endure discomfort and painful uncertainty in order to find the way that brings life to ourselves and others.

At the heart of the Quaker way is the discovery that we are made for love, for sharing, self-giving and rejoicing in the well-being of all people and the world of living beings. A life that is guided, shaped and surrendered to the Inward Guide is rich in meaning and significance, because it is poured out for others. The guided life is not a life of comfort, security or accumulation. It may lead us into substantial hardships and sacrifices. In some times and places, like seventeenth-century England or twentieth-century Rhodesia, it will lead to conflict and invite persecution. In every age, it will call us to let go of some of our self-centred cravings and cherished ambitions.

To nurture a relationship with the Inward Guide risks

inviting discomfort, trouble and sacrifice into our lives. Rather than ease and security, the Spirit offers life, in all its disturbing, challenging and abundant vitality. A life that is lived generously and open-heartedly, willing to take risks for the well-being of others and the flourishing of the world, is one that is charged with significance, even at those times when it is least apparent. Most of the consequences of our actions are never visible to us; we are constantly scattering seeds that affect those around us in ways we will never know about. As we allow our lives to be guided into the ways of divine compassion, we will become a blessing to others, and to the world around us, even without our knowing it.

The aim of living is not to creep through life with the minimum of discomfort. It is for each of us to become the person we were born to be; by giving ourselves, bringing into the world the unique gifts of beauty, friendship, compassion or creativity that only we can offer in this time and place. How we choose to respond to life's mysterious demands, how we bear our sufferings and live our daily lives is profoundly important. The world needs people who are willing to come fully alive, to become guided men and women. Each of us needs to nourish the Seed of life within us, to find the unique path that will enable our own contribution to the flourishing of the world. Your way will be very different from mine. I hope you will seek it out and live it.

Appendix

Experiment with Light

The 'Experiment with Light' is a form of guided meditation developed by Rex Ambler and a group of other modern Quakers, based on the discernment practice of early Quakers. It can be practised by individuals or in small groups, as an aid to developing our connection and relationship with the Inward Guide. There are several versions of the meditation; one of the simplest follows four basic steps, which are described below. Each step starts with a very short prompt being read out, followed by about six minutes of silence.

Mind the Light

Pay attention to your own awareness, to your capacity for clear perception of what is going on in your body, heart and mind. This capacity for awareness is the 'Light' that will show us what we need to know for our healing and maturity. It helps to pay attention to our posture; breathing slowly and gently, and taking time to allow the mind to settle. By allowing distracting thoughts to simply come and go and our minds to become still, we can bring our lives and concerns into the light of awareness; the Inward Light that can illuminate the areas where we need greater insight and guidance.

Open Yourself to the Light

In this condition of settled, attentive inward and outward stillness, bring to mind the concerns of your life right now. Focus on a particular area that needs more clarity or guidance. Without getting caught up in worries or speculations, just allow the issue to be present in your mind's eye. You may find you have a question connected with it, such as 'what is going on here?' or 'what needs to be done?' It helps to keep any question in mind without trying to answer it or work it out. Just stay interested and open to whatever might reveal itself.

Wait in the Light

Simply remain patiently open and attentive, without trying to generate solutions, holding the issue or question in the light of awareness. It may need patience and persistence to notice when the mind starts to wander, and bring it gently back to sit with the question. By staying with the issue in this way, you may find that an image, a word or a feeling seems to arise by itself, quite independently of your deliberate thinking.

The very simple process of holding a question in the light of awareness, without the operation of the rational, problem-solving part of the mind, allows the Inward Light to reveal aspects of it that we were previously unaware of. Often, this is expressed in the non-literal language of the deeper levels of consciousness; in symbolic images or words that may seem obscure and difficult to interpret. By sitting patiently with the images or words that come to you, and perhaps returning to them over several sittings, they will often reveal a new aspect of the situation, or point towards a new course of action.

Submit to the Light

The final part of the meditation is simply to accept with gratitude whatever has been shown to you by the Inward Light, to let it sink into your heart and mind, with a willingness to let yourself be guided by it. Whatever has come up in the meditation may raise further questions, and it can help to return to it repeatedly in an unfolding dialogue. It is often also helpful to share it with a trusted group of friends, who can offer support with any experiences that may be disturbing or challenging. This is often done as part of a local Experiment with Light group.

The guided meditations are available as recordings on the

Experiment with Light website, along with other useful guidance and resources at: www.experiment-with-light.org.uk

References

Chapter 1

Patricia Loring, *Spiritual Discernment: The Context and Goal of Clearness Committees*, Pendle Hill Pamphlet 305, 1992

Francis Howgill, *A lamentation for the scattered tribes*, 1656

Chapter 2

Isaac Penington, *Selections from the Works of Isaac Penington*, 1837

Alexander Parker, *A Manifestation of Divine Love*,1660

Isaac Penington, *A Brief Account Concerning Silent Meetings*, 1680

Gerald Hewitson, *Journey into Life: Inheriting the story of early Friends*, Swarthmore Lecture, 2013

Isaac Penington, *Some directions to the panting soul*, 1661

William Penn, *Some fruits of solitude*, 1693

Chapter 3

Isaac Penington, *Letters*, ed John Barclay, 1828

Timothy Ashworth & Alex Wildwood, *Rooted in Christianity, Open to New Light: Quaker Spiritual Diversity*, 2009.

Margaret Heathfield, *Being Together: Our Corporate Life in the Religious Society of Friends*, Swarthmore Lecture, 1994

Chapter 4

James Nayler, in *A collection of sundry books, epistles and papers*, 1716

John Macmurray, *Search for a Faith*, 1945

John Woolman, *Journal*, 1774

Isaac Penington, *Some directions to the Panting Soul*, 1661

George Fox, *Journal*, 1694

Chapter 5

Advices & Queries, *Quaker faith & practice*, 1995

William Taber, *Four Doors to Meeting for Worship*, Pendle Hill Pamphlet 306, 1992

Bernard Canter, editorial in *The Friend*, vol 120, 1962, p. 770

John Woolman, *Journal*, 1774

Thomas Moore, *The Re-Enchantment of Everyday Life*, 1996

A Declaration from the harmless and innocent people of God, called Quakers, in George Fox, *Journal*, 1694

Also in this series

Quaker Roots and Branches
John Lampen

Quaker Roots and Branches explores what Quakers call their 'testimonies' – the interaction of inspiration, faith and action to bring change in the world. It looks at Quaker concerns around the sustainability of the planet, peace and war, punishment, and music and the arts in the past and today. It stresses the continuity of their witness over three hundred and sixty-five years as well as their openness to change and development.

Telling the Truth about God
Rhiannon Grant

Telling the truth about God without excluding anyone is a challenge to the Quaker community. Drawing on the author's academic research into Quaker uses of religious language and her teaching to Quaker and academic groups, Rhiannon Grant aims to make accessible some key theological and philosophical insights. She explains that Quakers might sound vague but are actually making clear and creative theological claims.

What Do Quakers Believe?
Geoffrey Durham

Geoffrey Durham answers the crucial question 'What do Quakers believe?' clearly, straightforwardly and without jargon. In the process he introduces a unique religious group whose impact and influence in the world is far greater than their numbers suggest. *What Do Quakers Believe?* is a friendly, direct and accessible toe-in-the-water book for readers who have often wondered who these Quakers are, but have never quite found out.

THE NEW OPEN SPACES

Throughout the two thousand years of Christian tradition there
have been, and still are, groups and individuals that exist in
the margins and upon the edge of faith. But in Christianity's
contrapuntal history it has often been these outcasts and
pioneers that have forged contemporary orthodoxy out
of former radicalism as belief evolves to engage with and
encompass the ever-changing social and scientific realities. Real
faith lies not in the comfortable certainties of the Orthodox,
but somewhere in a half-glimpsed hinterland on the dirt track
to Emmaus, where the Death of God meets the Resurrection,
where the supernatural Christ meets the historical Jesus,
and where the revolution liberates both the oppressed and
the oppressors.

Welcome to Christian Alternative... a space at the edge where
the light shines through.
If you have enjoyed this book, why not tell other readers by
posting a review on your preferred book site.

Recent bestsellers from Christian Alternative are:

Bread Not Stones
The Autobiography of An Eventful Life
Una Kroll
The spiritual autobiography of a truly remarkable woman
and a history of the struggle for ordination in the Church of
England.
Paperback: 978-1-78279-804-0 ebook: 978-1-78279-805-7

The Quaker Way
A Rediscovery
Rex Ambler
Although fairly well known, Quakerism is not well understood.
The purpose of this book is to explain how Quakerism works as
a spiritual practice.
Paperback: 978-1-78099-657-8 ebook: 978-1-78099-658-5

Blue Sky God
The Evolution of Science and Christianity
Don MacGregor
Quantum consciousness, morphic fields and blue-sky
thinking about God and Jesus the Christ.
Paperback: 978-1-84694-937-1 ebook: 978-1-84694-938-8

Celtic Wheel of the Year
Tess Ward
An original and inspiring selection of prayers combining
Christian and Celtic Pagan traditions, and interweaving their
calendars into a single pattern of prayer for every morning
and night of the year.
Paperback: 978-1-90504-795-6

Christian Atheist
Belonging without Believing
Brian Mountford
Christian Atheists don't believe in God but miss him: especially
the transcendent beauty of his music, language, ethics, and
community.
Paperback: 978-1-84694-439-0 ebook: 978-1-84694-929-6

Compassion Or Apocalypse?
A Comprehensible Guide to the Thoughts of René Girard
James Warren
How René Girard changes the way we think about God and the Bible, and its relevance for our apocalypse-threatened world.
Paperback: 978-1-78279-073-0 ebook: 978-1-78279-072-3

Diary Of A Gay Priest
The Tightrope Walker
Rev. Dr. Malcolm Johnson
Full of anecdotes and amusing stories, but the Church is still a dangerous place for a gay priest.
Paperback: 978-1-78279-002-0 ebook: 978-1-78099-999-9

Do You Need God?
Exploring Different Paths to Spirituality Even For Atheists
Rory J.Q. Barnes
An unbiased guide to the building blocks of spiritual belief.
Paperback: 978-1-78279-380-9 ebook: 978-1-78279-379-3

Readers of ebooks can buy or view any of these bestsellers by clicking on the live link in the title. Most titles are published in paperback and as an ebook. Paperbacks are available in traditional bookshops. Both print and ebook formats are available online.

Find more titles and sign up to our readers' newsletter at
http://www.johnhuntpublishing.com/christianity
Follow us on Facebook at
https://www.facebook.com/ChristianAlternative